DODGING DISASTER

TIPS AND TRICKS FOR RAISING YOUR TEENAGED DAUGHTER AS A SINGLE DAD

OLIVER B. HARTE JR

Co-Authored by

Malika Hill

Reality Set In

So, there I was at the age of thirty-three years old all alone with a teenage daughter. After several years of attempting to make a marriage work, her mom and I decided that we would pursue separate lives. I'll be the first to admit that I was surprised when she suggested that our daughter stay with me. Typically, this isn't the case in separating couples but hey, this was my kid, I loved her to the moon and back and I didn't have a problem with it at all. My then wife decided that she was going to take the opportunity to travel a bit and eventually settle and work in Europe for a while. Her decision did not sit too well with me, but I could not stop her. So, three months into our separation she booked a plane ticket, said goodbye to our daughter and took off.

As my daughter and I drove back home from the airport my mind began to ponder what life will be like. Raising a child is incredibly challenging for anyone, I had no idea how much more it would be for myself. Historically, I was the one that was always gone. My wife was the one who stayed home, well, locally anyway, and took care of our. This change was going to be quite challenging for me. I did not realize how challenging though, until the next morning when I woke up to a quiet house. This was a bit strange because typically I would hear the coffee machine going, or CNN in the background or some other noise. It was quiet because the noise makers were not around. My wife was now gone, and my daughter spent what was supposed to be our first night alone over at her friend's house.

I laid in bed for a bit, allowing my mind to wander. Remembering back to when she was just a little girl how the simplest things used to amaze her. She was so full of wonder and imagination that it made me smile. Recently though, as she turned into a teenager, it seemed as though she was more interested in ticking her mom and I off than anything else. Clearly, I do not actually believe that, but it is just how it seemed. I am not certain what happens when little girls become teenagers, but they become extremely moody and sometimes disrespectful. Before I knew it I began to feel overwhelmed and I wasn't even out of bed yet!

It was only about 7:00 a.m. on a Saturday morning so I knew my dad was on his daily stroll around the community him and my mom lived in. I picked up my phone, scrolled to his contact, pressed his face and called him. When the phone rang the first thing I heard my father say jokingly was "you change your mind yet son?"

He was referring to the offer he made earlier in the week to have his granddaughter stay with him and my mom for the summer. I chuckled and politely replied "no dad, just calling to say hi." Our conversations were usually quick and succinct. They never lasted more than four or five minutes. This time however I found myself rambling on and on mindlessly about different things. My dad finally asked me what was on my mind and why I had called. I finally got around to telling him how overwhelmed I began to feel, and it had only been one night. I guess I really did not have a reason to feel this way just yet, but it was definitely coming. My dad did what he always does. He encouraged me and told me that everything was going to be all right. After a few more minutes on the phone I said goodbye and hung up. I decided to get out of bed and go for a run. It was just after sunrise and it was a beautiful day. I decided to listen to some music while I ran to take my mind away from the situation. As I ran however, I realized that I was not listening to the music at all, but my mind was wandering erratically. I started making plans for my daughter and I that summer. I figured we would go visit my parents, then I thought about taking her down to Florida. I even thought about taking her to Europe to visit her mom but quickly dismissed that idea. The separation was still fresh and there was still a lot of hard feelings and anxiety. I thought best to dismiss the idea quickly.

Towards the end of my run my daughter called and asked if I could pick her up early so she could get a change of clothes to head back out with her friends. I had known her friends and their parents since the girls were much younger and had never had any issues with allowing her to spend time with them. I agreed and went about my day.

Later on that evening when she was getting ready to go back to her friend's house, I popped into her room and saw her in the mirror putting on makeup. It caught me a little off guard because this was the first time, I had seen this. I did not even know she was at this point yet. About a year ago I had gotten a promotion at work, but the new position required me to travel extensively so I was almost never around. I knew that there were some changes she was bound to go through but I did not think my little princess was at the point where she was putting on makeup. Looks like I missed a lot.

I didn't quite know what to say. Her mom and I had never had this discussion. At least not that I remember. I asked her if she was ready, to which she replied, "in a few minutes dad". I headed out to wait for her in the car. A few minutes later she came outside dressed in a skirt I did not know she had, a face full of makeup and what looked like a small suitcase. The skirt is what threw me off. It was way too short for someone her age and inappropriate in my opinion. Before she reached the car, I got out and stopped her dead in her tracks.

"Excuse me young lady, but where do you think you're going dressed like that?"
"Like what?" She asked.
I asked her where she got the skirt from because I don't think her mom would have bought it for her and I know I definitely had not.

"It's one of Vanessa's. She let me hold it for tonight." She said.
"You're thirteen years old. Go change!" I replied hastily.

I promptly asked her to return to her room, take it off and put on something a little more age appropriate. This is when I realized that my little girl had turned into a fire breathing dragon at some point over the past few years and I had never realized it. She did not say anything. At least not audibly, but I definitely heard her murmur something to herself as she turned around, stormed back into the house and slammed the door behind her. I almost yelled out loud but did not. Our house was pretty close to the neighbors and I did not want them peeking through the blinds. I followed her back inside period when I got to her bedroom the door was closed. I knocked but she did not answer. I knocked again, still no answer. I reached for the handle to open it when it flew open.

"Is this better FATHER!?" She yelled.

This was when I realized I was in trouble......

Not Easy, But Achievable

Simply put, there is no guidebook to parenting. Raising a child alone can be tough for anyone. Studies show that more and more kids are living in single parent households. As of 2019, there were 15.76 million children living with their single mothers while 3.23 million children were living with their single fathers (Zuckerman, 2020). However, raising a teenage daughter as a single dad can be exceptionally tough. As a father and a man, it can be a struggle connecting with and understanding your teenage daughter. No matter how much parents detest it, the teenage years and the reckless emotions that come with those years are inevitable. In order to raise a teenage daughter, parents must first understand that it is hard being a teenage girl. Teenage girls face an unnerving range of stressors that can potentially put them at risk for developing self-harming behaviors like abusing drugs, developing eating disorders, anxiety, and even depression (Hemmen, 2012).

The purpose of this book is to briefly explore the challenges single dads face while raising their daughters into adulthood. This book will address the teenage development process and explore developmental milestones for teenage girls. Also, it will present some of the main stressors faced by teenage girls. Additionally, we will discuss why active fathers matter and what some of the common struggles faced by single dads raising daughters who are rapidly approaching adulthood can be. Lastly, this article will provide some tips and tricks for single dads raising teenage daughters. A survey of over 200 different men who are all raising teenage daughters was given in order to conduct much of this research.

Separation Anxiety

My ex-wife's decision to move abroad seemed to come out of nowhere and definitely caught myself and my daughter off guard. Of course, being physically separated for quite some time, I was used to not having her around, but our daughter was still able to have our relationship with both of her parents and saw us both daily. It was not until the end of the summer after we'd taken her to the airport that I started to notice some strange behavior from my daughter.

Kids tend to handle separation anxiety a little different than adults do. Some of the things that started to happen were... Her grades started to slip, she became disruptive in class, she tried staying home from school and even skipping a few times. Then there were physical symptoms. The headaches, stomach aches, waking up during the middle of the night and complaining about dreams of her mom dying, insomnia seemed to be a big one. In general, she began to shy away from all the things she loved, like cheerleading and track practice. Another one was panic attacks. From my days as an undergrad while studying psychology, I recognized some of these symptoms. Of course, when I was faced with them directly I had no clue what was going on. It wasn't until I sat down with a therapist and began to discuss the situation with her, that I realized what was actually happening period my daughter was going through separation anxiety, and from the looks of it, a severe case.

I decided to attempt to become a bit more active in her life. Instead of being condescending and judgmental like some parents tend to do, I took an interest into things she still showed an interest in period She didn't always feel like it, but we went for frequent walks together in the evenings after dinner physical touch is very important. I consistently embraced her and reassured her that her mom still loves her. I did my best to make sure they communicated as often as possible. This did not solve the issues overnight, but it began to slowly take effect. over the course of a few months I realized that there was a reversal in her behavior period her grades went back up and she once again showed an interest in the things she loved. It was not easy at all, but it had to start somewhere.

Sometimes as a single dad, you'll find yourself in situations you weren't prepared for. Of course, this isn't going to cover every scenario, but the following few items will at least get you started on the path to getting through someone comfortable moments you'll most certainly run into raising a teenage girl.

Fatherhood in America is Changing

Research suggests that more and more fathers are taking on a more active role in the lives of their children. The current generation of children have seen an incredible increase in the number of single fathers. Historically, women have been the primary caretakers. It is not uncommon for a child to be raised by a single mother. However, fatherhood in America is changing. A 2016 study showed that single dads made up 17% of all stay-at-home parents which is up from 10% in 1989 (Livingston & Parker, 2019). That gradual increase can be attributed to the fact that today's fathers now see parenting as an important part to their identity (Livingston & Parker, 2019). The purpose of this section is to provide some discuss the changing landscape of parenthood and the impact fathers have on their children.

Like many mothers, fathers seem to also appreciate the experience of parenthood. Based on a survey done by Pew Research Center, 54% of single dads reported that parenting is rewarding all the time (Livingston & Parker, 2019). Single dads also face some of the same struggles as single moms such as juggling work and family life, financial pressure, and the overall feeling of just not doing enough. Based on a 2015 research survey of single dads, half of the dads, 52%, admitted that balancing work and family life is somewhat hard (Livingston & Parker, 2019). Additionally, about three-in-ten working dads (29%) said they "always feel rushed," (Livingston & Parker, 2019). In 2017 survey, 76% of adults inferred that men face an immense amount of pressure to financially support their families (Livingston & Parker, 2019). Lastly, while more dads are becoming more active in their parenting, 63% felt like they still did not spend enough time with their children (Livingston & Parker, 2019). Moreover, research suggests that some single dads are not confident in their overall parenting style. Only 39% felt they were doing their best to raise their kids (Livingston & Parker, 2019). Below are two charts by the Pew Research Center. The first chart illustrates the importance of childhood to both parents. The second chart illustrates how single moms and dads feel about balancing their work and personal lives.

For many working dads, balancing work and family is a challenge

% saying it is very/somewhat difficult to balance the reponsibilities of work and family

Dads	52%
Moms	60

% saying they are always rushed

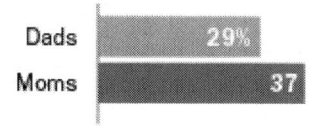

Dads	29%
Moms	37

Note: Based on all full- or part-time working parents.
Source: Pew Research Center survey of parents with children under 18, Sept. 15-Oct. 13, 2015

PEW RESEARCH CENTER

Based on this chart it is evident that both mothers and fathers find balancing work and personal responsibilities challenging. However, these challenges do not change how they feel about parenting. This is proven in the following chart.

Fatherhood a positive experience and central to dads' identity

% saying parenting is extremely important to their identity

Dads	57%
Moms	58

% saying parenting is rewarding all of the time

Dads	54%
Moms	52

% saying parenting is enjoyable all of the time

Dads	46%
Moms	41

Source: Pew Research Center survey of parents with children under 18, Sept.15-Oct.13, 2015

PEW RESEARCH CENTER

This chart shows that even though it may be challenging to find that perfect balance, both mothers and fathers define parenting as a positive and fulfilling experience. This chart also shows that dads actually enjoy parenting a little bit more than some mothers. Even though most dads find parenting enjoyable, they still feel they are not doing enough.

Tips and tricks for raising your teenaged daughter as a single dad

About six-in-ten dads say they spend too little time with their kids ...

% of parents of children younger than age 18 who say they spend _____ time with their children

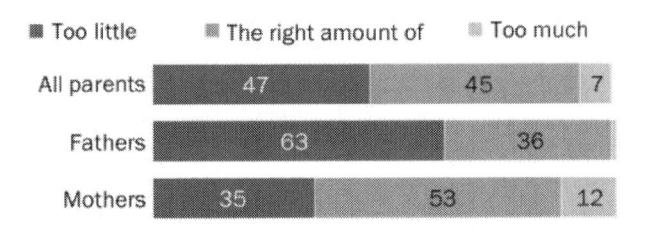

- Too little
- The right amount of
- Too much

	Too little	The right amount of	Too much
All parents	47	45	7
Fathers	63	36	
Mothers	35	53	12

... mostly due to work obligations

% who say _____ is the main reason for spending too little time with their children, among parents who say they spend too little time with their children

- Work obligations
- Children too busy with other activities
- Children don't live with them all the time
- Other family or household obligations

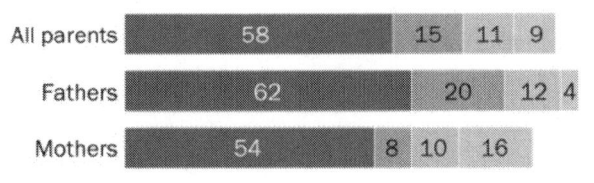

	Work	Don't live with	Too busy	Other
All parents	58	15	11	9
Fathers	62	20	12	4
Mothers	54	8	10	16

Notes: Based on parents ages 18 and older. In the top chart, values of 1% or less are not shown. In the bottom chart, those who gave some other answer are not shown.
Source: Survey of U.S. adults conducted Aug. 8-21 and Sept. 14-28, 2017.

PEW RESEARCH CENTER

This chart, also by the Pew Research Institute, illustrates how dads feel about their parenting skills as compared to mothers. Based on this chart, single dads feel like they do not spend enough time with their children which is largely due to work constraints. On the other hand, the single mothers in this survey felt like they spent too much time with their children.

Being an Active Father

Despite what some fathers may think, they are needed in order to raise a healthy and balanced child. The relationship a child has with their fathers can impact the relationship they have not only with other people, but themselves as well. Research suggests that a father's involvement in their children's lives has a positive effect on their child's wellbeing in many different ways. According to the CDC, father involvement increases the chances of academic and career success and decreases the chances of substance abuse and delinquency (Jones & Mosher, 2013). Researchers also infer that regular positive contact with a father reduces criminal behavior (Krisch, 2020). This is especially true among low-income families. Additionally, father involvement enhances cognitive skills in children.

Children with an involved father have also been known to have higher self-control, self-discipline, social competence and also empathy (Krisch, 2020). Girls who have active fathers are less likely to develop bad relationship patterns such as staying in an abusive relationship. They will look for good qualities in their spouses because of the examples they had in their fathers. Additionally, girls with active fathers are less likely to take sexual risks such as engaging in sex at an early age.

Single Dads Need Help Also

Although the percentage of single dads is still relatively lower than single moms, they are equally just as important. There are frequent dreads among single fathers. For example, some may fear that if the mother comes back into the child's life that she will try to regain or take full custody. Additionally, some single dads feel like they are not good enough, especially when it comes to raising a teenage daughter. However, statistically, an active father is equally important.

Development Process

No matter how much parents detest it, the teenage years and the reckless emotions that come with those years are inevitable. This could very well be one of the hardest stages of parenting. Teen development, also known as adolescent development, can be defined as the transition period between childhood and adulthood. It is important for single dads to understand the development process their teenage daughter is going through. This in turn will help single dads everywhere understand their daughters and the various emotions they go through as they make that change from adolescence into adulthood. The purpose of this section is to briefly discuss the development process for teenage girls.

Developmental Milestones for Teenage Girls

It is a scientific fact that girls mature faster than boys. The onset of menstruation marks the beginning of puberty for girls. Once a girl begins menstruating regularly, she is capable of reproduction. Girls will normally go through puberty when they are between 8 and 13 years old. (Johnson, 2018). Typically, the first change your teenage daughter will experience is growth of breast tissue. As she gets older, your teenager will also begin to grow hair in the pubic region and eventually under her arms. Your daughter's body shape will also change a lot, with her hips becoming wider and her waist becoming narrower. She will also grow taller and heavier. Personal hygiene is important during this period. Make sure she has the necessary smell goods like deodorant and lotion. Additionally, your daughter may have her first period any time between 10 and 16 years old (scary right?) Research suggests that this generation of young girls have begun to get their cycles a lot earlier than other generations (Johnson, 2018). Therefore, the earlier you educate your daughter on her changing body, the better.

Why Understanding Teen Development is Important

Teen development, also known as adolescence, is important to understand. This is largely because if you understand why your teenage daughter acts a certain way, you will know how to deal with the different behaviors and emotions she will display in a positive way. Adolescence is an important time in your daughter's life. It's a time to develop knowledge and skills, learn to manage emotions and relationships, and acquire attributes and abilities that will be important for enjoying the adolescent years and assuming adult roles (Clinic, 2020). As your daughter begins to go through puberty, she will likely be a little more confrontational as she sifts through her changing and growing body. Understanding teen development is also important to understand because during this time period, children start developing their own identity. Your teenage daughter will start to develop a strong sense of self and a connection to others. She will crave her own since of individuality. A teenager's identity can be the result of internal and external factors as well as external forces such as their siblings, peers, families, and ethnic identities (Watson, 2019). Most of these factors and forces are out of their control. Research suggests that a positive self-identity is correlated with high self esteem (Watson, 2019).

What is Teen Development?

Teen development is tricky, and it is not the same for everyone. Teen development, also known as adolescent development, can be defined as the transition period between childhood and adulthood. An adolescent is any person between ages 10 and 19 (Csikszentmihalyi). The stages of adolescence include: early adolescence from ages 10 to 14; mid-adolescence from ages 15 to 17, and late adolescence from ages 18 to 24 (Johnson, 2018). Adolescence is one of the most important phases of our lives. During these years, children go through different physical, intellectual, personal, and social changes.

Physical Changes

As mentioned earlier, it is a scientific fact that girls mature faster than boys. These changes include but are not limited to growth spurts, puberty, and bodily signs of sexual maturity, like growing hair in places where there was none originally. For girls, the onset of menstruation marks the beginning of puberty. There is not a set age that girls will begin having regular cycles, however, it is important to educate them on what to expect in case you are not around. It is also important to educate your teenage daughter about menstruation because once a girl begins to menstruate regularly; she is capable of reproduction.

Intellectual Changes

In addition to the physical changes your teenage daughter will go through, she will also go through intellectual changes. This means that she will start to think differently. Most teens can think abstractly which separates them from children. Your teenager will learn to consider different possibilities, conduct reasoning from their own principles, and consider that there are infinite possibilities (Clinic, 2020). Intellectual changes also mean that your teenager will start to challenge you more as they begin to learn and reason. Not all intellectual changes happen at once (thank Goodness).

Personal Changes

As your child continues to develop into a young adult, her personality will likely change. Your teenager's personality may change according to the situation or her group of friends. Understanding your teenager's personality traits will help you easily predict how they will react in certain situations. Research studies show that an individual's personality stabilizes as people reach adulthood (Markman, 2017).

Social and Emotional Changes

Teenage girls go through a rollercoaster of emotional changes as they navigate towards adulthood. As your teenage daughter continues to grow, she will likely spend more time with her peers and less time with her family as she tries to form her own identity. Additionally, your teenage daughter will start to become more socially aware. Social media has become a huge part of the lives of teenagers everywhere. Social media enables teenagers to create their own identity online and build social networks. Although there are many benefits of social media, it can also negatively affect teens. Social media can become a distraction and expose your teenager to various forms of bullying. Therefore, it is important to keep an eye on your daughter's social media use.

Being a Teenager Is Stressful

There is no guidebook to parenting. Most parents learn through trial and error. After all, experience is the best teacher. All parents really want to do is protect their children and help them navigate through this crazy world in the safest, smartest, and lucrative way. The older your child or children get, the more challenges you will likely face as a parent. Just the thought of these challenges can be really daunting. Things like teen pregnancy and STD statistics can cause parents to become overly protective of their children causing a distrusting relationship. Simply put, this is not the best idea because you cannot protect your child from everything that the world throws at them. Parents can only prepare their children for the challenges they may face not fight them themselves.

In order to raise a teenage daughter, parents must first understand that it is hard being a teenage girl. Today's teenage girls are exposed to a lot of things some good and some bad. Furthermore, teenage girls face an unnerving range of stressors that can potentially put them at risk for developing self-harming behaviors like abusing drugs, developing eating disorders, anxiety, and even depression (Hemmen, 2012). The purpose of this section is to discuss the stressors that teenage girls incur on a day to day basis. Such stressors include but are not limited to:

➢ Schools and Grades

According to a recent case study done on the top stressors for teenage girls, researchers found that the top stressor for teenage girls include getting good grades, getting into extracurricular activities, and of course getting into college (Magher, 2017). Furthermore, maintaining friendships and social status can also increase stress levels for teenage girls. Every parent wants their kids to excel in school so unknowingly, parents do apply pressure. However, the best thing to do would be to encourage your teenager to try her best rather than be the best.

➢ Family Issues

Following behind school, studies show that family life has a big impact on the stress levels of teenage girls. Based on a study done by the Cincinnati Children's Hospital, having a family history of substance abuse, parental separation, major illness, or poor family communication are all top stressors for teen girls (Magher, 2017). Furthermore, studies show that teens named their younger siblings as a stressor. Sibling rivalry and family expectations that a teen caring for younger children can also contribute towards high stress levels. Also, some teenagers may stress over feeling like she has to compete with her sibling or siblings for affection or validation.

➢ Body Image

Teenage girls are constantly under pressure to adapt to social ideals of beauty. This is something that has been going on for years. Teenage girls can become obsessed with maintaining a certain weight so they can look like the girls they see on tv and in magazines. Growing girls will go through body changes and it is important to let your teenager know that it is completely normal and natural for their weight to fluctuate. Body image stress could cause tiredness in your teen and worsen their mental health. That is why it is important to tell your teenage daughter how beautiful they are every day just the way they are.

➢ New Romances and Changes

Early teenage relationships often involve exploring intimacy and sexual feelings. While you might not feel ready for this, it is inevitable. There is no set time or age for teenage girls to begin desiring a romantic relationship with the opposite sex, every child is different. Parents have an important role in guiding and supporting their teenage daughters through this important developmental stage. Teenage girls sometimes can have a hard time sifting through varying emotions especially when they involve the opposite sex. As your teenage daughter gets older, it is natural for her to be attracted to the opposite sex and this can lead to a lot of changes in her behavior. For example, she may take extra time getting ready in the morning or go out of her way to tell you about someone she is interested in. Of course, this can cause a lot of stress on both you as the parent and your teenage daughter. Teenage girls may feel pressured to engage in sexual activities when they are not ready, may be confused about what they want in the relationship; or may even be figuring out how to deal with bad treatment from a partner (Magher, 2017). Parents may feel pressured to ground their daughter until she is 60 to prevent the extra stress. However, it is up to you, the parent, to be there for your daughter while she is sifting through her romantic feelings.

➤ Finances

Of course most teenage girls do not have actual bills like you and me. However, they may feel pressured to have the top designer shoes and wear expensive clothing in order to keep up with the latest trends. Most teenagers have the desire to want to look "cool" in front of their peers. When their family can't provide these things, this creates stress. Teens can also be affected by financial stress experienced by their parents, especially if it results in things like a move or scarcity in food or other necessities (Magher, 2017). It is important to teach your teenage daughter financial responsibility. If you are able to provide her with an allowance where she can do a service around the house for money, do it. Encourage her to make and save her own money so she can save to purchase the extra things she wants.

➤ Cyber Bullying

This is a new but very common stressor amongst teenage girls (Magher, 2017). Research attests that cyber bullying is on the rise. In a study done by the National Center for Education Statistics, cyber bullying increased among teens

3.5 percent since the 2014-2015 school year (Gills, 2020). Cyber bullying should be treated just the same as regular bullying. The effects of cyber bullying can be just as destructive and stressful. Parents should counsel and monitor their teenagers on their use of the Internet.

Common Struggles that Fathers Raising Teenage Daughters Face

Parenting can become extremely daunting for single fathers involved with raising teenage daughters. A single parent can be defined as a parent who exercises parenthood alone, without the support of the other parent (Pace, 2020). Becoming a single dad can be a result of circumstances which may include some of the following

- *Death of the mother*
- *Irresponsibility of the mother*
- *Divorce*
- *Unintended pregnancy*
- *Single parent adoption*

Raising a teenage daughter as a single dad comes with unique situations and challenges. This can be attributed to the fact that the social experiences, feelings, and developmental changes teenage girls go through most single dads cannot understand or relate to (Myers, 2019).

Most moms can remember dealing with a plethora of emotions as their bodies began to change and in some cases were not comfortable verbalizing their feelings and emotions, especially to their fathers. They, therefore, know the trials and tribulations teenage girls go through, so they can relate. However, this is not the case for single dads. While every father and daughter will face their own challenges, opportunities, and success, there are a few common struggles that fathers raising teenage daughters alone face. The purpose of this section is to describe some of the struggle single dads face.

Being Neutral in Mother Daughter Disagreements

Having a cordial relationship with the mother of your child is a critical part towards raising a teenage daughter as a single dad. If you have that luxury, take advantage. Additionally, staying neutral in mother daughter disputes is also necessary to keep the peace between a mother and her teenage daughter. Staying neutral also improves trust between you and your daughter. It is no secret that there is typically a power struggle between a mother and her teenage daughter. Therefore, it is important for you, her father, to stay neutral and not pick sides. If you side with your daughter, you will create a rift between yourself and the mother of your child. If you side with the mother of your child, it could hurt the relationship you have with your daughter. So, stay neutral!

Having the Birds and the Bee's Talk

Now this may be very difficult for many fathers. It is hard to accept that your little girl is growing up into a woman. However, it is inevitable. Do NOT skip the birds and the bees talk. No matter how uncomfortable it is, it is important for your teenage daughter to hear it from you. It just resonates differently. Do not leave it all up to mom. It is more relaxing if you and the mother of your daughter had the talk together to show your teenager that she has a strong support system that will always support her.

Understanding that Boyfriends are Ok

Admittedly, this is a tough one for most dads, especially me. When little girls become teenagers, most start really liking boys. Even worse, they want to date them. For most fathers, this can be a terrifying and enraging part of raising their teenage daughter, especially if they are doing it alone. A lot of men fear their daughters being used or played by a teenage boy which makes it hard to trust or allow a teenage boy around your daughter. However, it does not negate the fact that boyfriends are inevitable as your teenage daughter becomes a young adult. Teenage girls tend to spend an exceptional amount of time thinking and talking about being in a relationship. The great thing about these teenage relationships is that they might last only a few weeks or months. On the contrary, it is also normal for your teenage daughter to have no interest in romantic relationships until their late teens.

Staying Involved

As your teenage daughter gets older, she will begin to assert her own independence from her family, especially her father. It is important to remember that this is a necessary part of growth, so don't take it personal. I know that is way easier said than done but it is important that you give her room to breathe while keeping a close eye on her daily activities. This helps build a trusting relationship between you and your daughter.

Dealing with A Distant Teenager

Part of growing up and becoming an adult is asserting independence from parents and family members. Knowing that it's a necessary aspect of your teen daughter's development doesn't make it any less painful though. Watching your daughter make a concerted effort to push you away or isolate herself is both difficult and hurtful. However, it is something that every father must face.

Understanding the Power of your Presence

Fathers have an extraordinary impact on their daughter's self-esteem. It is said that a little girl's father is her first love. Studies show that when fathers are absent, their daughters are affected in many negative ways both physically and emotionally (Jones & Mosher, 2013). However, when they are present and loving, their daughters develop a strong sense of security and become more confident in themselves overall. The Father Effect suggests that girls who are fortunate enough to have dads in their lives excel and potentially outperform their peers (Krisch, 2020).

Open Lines of Communication

Research shows that while this can be hard and uncomfortable at first, having open communication with your teenage daughter will likely keep her out of a lot of trouble (Rice, 2020). Most many tend to listen long enough to identify the problem and the solution. That is not what your daughter wants. Instead of solving her problem, your teenage daughter just wants to vent to you without any judgment or backlash. Now, I know this is easier said than done. However, single dads should learn to be compassionate and empathetic to their daughter's problems, even if you do not quite understand or agree. This will show your daughter that she has a shoulder to lean on. Of course, this will take time and a whole lot of patience but creating open lines of communication will benefit both you and your teenage daughter.

Daddy-Daughter Life Hacks

1. Problem solving skills

Do your best to avoid the temptation to solve every problem your dog has. This should be set for children in general, but it's especially applicable to daughters. As dads, especially active ones, we tend to want to rush to the rescue and play the hero. This is okay to a certain degree but knowing when to let her find solutions to her own challenges is essential. Otherwise, you run the risk of having her think that everything works itself out and all she has to do is make some noise when she's faced with adversity. Instead of coddling her, sit with her and help her to identify what the issue actually is, then work through different ideas. It's okay to leave her, but not give her the answers all the time period it might seem frustrating at first, but once you've gotten her into the habit of consistently coming up with solutions on her own, I believe you'll find that it helps her to develop some self-confidence in this area. It's very essential to do this while she's a young teenager. One of the most dangerous things for a woman is to enter adulthood with low self-esteem and no confidence. In short, stop doing things for your daughter that she can do for herself.

2. Correction vs punishment

For many of us, we grew up being spanked or placed in time out when we misbehaved as children. A lot of the time we were punished when we should have been corrected. I think it goes without saying that in most cases for children, their misdeeds require corrective measures instead of being penalized. Daughters will push you. They will do that because to some degree society has instilled in them from very young that they are princesses and can get away with things. It is not easy to break that habit given the onslaught of influences from television, magazines, social media etc. It is up to us to train our daughters to respect authority and to challenge it respectfully when necessary.

It is important to associate the corrective measure you take with the misdeed period for example, if your daughter decides to skip class, then the correction for that should have to do with schooling in somehow. Whether it is doing extra assignments, staying late in detention, or even being made to tutor. The association definitely needs to be made and it needs to be done almost immediately. Punishing a child two or three weeks later for something that happens today does not have the effect we hope it will, because they have disassociated it with their actions and will only add some resentment to the mix. When they are much younger, timeout works, but at some point, it's no longer effective period what you do? Here are some things that seemed to work well for us.

➢ Chores

I had my daughter go to her aunt's house and do all her cousins' chores during what would normally be her free time. I did this in response to her slipping on her own chores or ignoring them all together. She did not think it was fair, but it quickly corrected her behavior.

➢ Bedtime was moved up.

I had never really liked the idea of having a television in her bedroom, but I ended up conceding one year and getting her one for Christmas. However, whenever she misbehaved, it took away the power cord and sent her to her room and forbade her from having anything to do in there except to spend the time thinking. No books, no electronics, no telephone, no nothing. She usually ended up falling asleep much sooner than her actual bedtime.

➢ Writing

I had actually learned this one from my 7th grade music teacher. Anytime someone in the class misbehaves or did not turn in an assignment on time, he would make us write enormous articles on the most inane and uninteresting subjects ever. I adopted this with my daughter when she was eleven and kept it up well into her teenage years. I would choose a subject at random and have her sit for what seemed like hours and write. Over the course of time it helped her improve her grammar tremendously.

3. Stress Relief

I know this one might seem a bit odd, but the truth is, most teenage girls go through an enormous amount of stress that they sometimes hide well because of peer pressure. It is important to identify this and do your best to help her alleviate it as much as possible. It is very important to have her around people she can trust as often as possible. It is also very important to emphatic. Remember what it was that helps her be happy and attempt to do those things. For my daughter, it was board games and ice cream. Of course, these two did not fix every problem she had, but it helped reset her mind to a place and time where she felt completely safe and secure. Stress often comes from not being able to see a solution to a challenge, so assisting her to work through any problems she may be facing will help greatly.

4. Avoid shallow praise and baseless flattery

When it comes to social media and the influences from outside your home, one of the most dangerous things that can happen is your daughter becomes too used to getting unearned compliments and unnecessary baseless flattery. These things do not help build self-esteem whatsoever. They only help her to become selfish and entitled. It is not always necessary to be the center of attention and can potentially be very dangerous if she is always made to feel as though she is without having earned it. Your daughter is your princess, and you should treat her as one, but princesses have responsibilities, and they are not just praised and respected because they were born into privilege. At least that is not how it is supposed to be. Teach her to command attention instead of just demanding it.

5. Understanding and Dealing with Failure

Providing your daughter with everything she asks for is dangerous. She will eventually develop a sense of entitlement and think she deserves everything she wants without working for it. Protecting her from failure at every turn is not doing her any good either. She will need to learn that life is not perfect and there will be missteps. The idea is that as a young lady she learns how to handle them and learn from her mistakes. Speaking of which, one of the worst ones I made with her was never allowing her to fall while learning to ride a bicycle. Every time she took off, I would run just behind her with one hand on the back of her seat and the other one poised to grab her. Every time she began to fall, I would snatch her off the bicycle and let it fall. She would never touch the ground, not once. I did not see the danger in this at the time, because I felt I was protecting my little girl. The problem was, she got too use to the feeling of invincibility. A few years after that while riding through our neighborhood and not paying attention to where she was going, the front wheel hit the sidewalk and she tumbled hard. This was the first time she had ever fallen off her bicycle and did not know how to handle it. The shame, the aggravation, the pain. She just sat there and cried for what seemed like hours. I watched the whole thing happened and felt terrible about it, because she did not know how to handle herself after that and was not used to working through that sort of pain and embarrassment. It was my own fault. Of course, as a parent you never wish to see your child injured and you'll do what you can to protect them, but failure is a part of life and having them develop the unrealistic expectation that it won't happen to them does them no good.

6. Decision Making

I often teach and coach that decision making is a skill that needs to be developed like anything else. This is especially important for teenage girls. At this age they enter a phase of their lives where they are prone to peer pressure and can find themselves in disastrous situations for making bad decisions. It is important to start training them to think beyond their actions. I helped my daughter process all the way through from the thought to the consequence. If she thinks she is not going to like what the result will be, it is probably best to avoid the action in the first place. Of course, this is not the easiest thing to do with your daughter, but constant reinforcement helps. Throughout her adolescence I constantly reminded her that in most cases, the lives we as adults have today is a direct result of the decisions we have made every day up until yesterday. If you like the trajectory in which it is headed, then do not make any changes. Do exactly what you have been doing. But if for some reason you dislike the direction you are heading in, then it is important to identify what decisions you have made that may need to change. Remind her that she may get to choose her actions, but she does not get to choose the consequences. We are often reminded of this during teenage pregnancy. I have never used it as a scare tactic, but as an effective tool. We visited several women's shelters and spoken to numerous young mothers who express the importance of learning how to properly make decisions as a young woman. I do not think anything else I could have done would have been more effective.

7. Learn How to Do her Hair (Just a little bit)

Cannot stress this enough. As silly as this sounds to most grown men, you will often find yourself in a situation where her hair is a mess and no one's around to help. Start from young. Get her used to the idea that her dad cares about her. You can do this without spending tons of money buying her things she does not need all the time. At first, you will be terrible at it, but that's nothing a few YouTube videos can't fix. What is most important is that the time you spend together will help her build trust in you as her protector and her provider. It will also instill in her the value for being resourceful. Lastly though, it will help her feel important and as though she were a priority, which she totally is! Of course, as she ages, she probably won't want you to do it anymore going into her teenage years but what will stick is the relationship you'll build when you set aside time specifically for this. My daughter would never let me touch her hair these days but the time we spent together was exceptionally valuable. During our sessions we would talk about everything from schoolwork to sports to social media. I have even gotten her to open up to me about boys, all during the time I spent with my hand in her head tugging helplessly at her scalp. It brought us closer together for certain. Almost half of the single dads that were interviewed for this article admitted to learning how to do hair. This is not necessarily a requirement, but the typical girl does not play about their hair. If you cannot learn how to do it, then get it done. This increases your daughter's self-esteem and also reduces the pressures of school stress.

Some Dad Rules to Follow

Raising a child alone can be tough for anyone. However, raising a teenage daughter as a single dad can be exceptionally tough because as a father and a man, it can be a struggle connecting with your teenage daughter. If you have strong women in your life like a sister, a mother, a friend, it would be wise to have them connect with your teenager. Sometimes it is just easier for girls to open up to girls. It is typical to see a single mom raising a daughter. It is easier for them because they can relate to the different challenges and emotions teenage girls go through. Now, that does not mean a man cannot successfully raise his daughter to be a strong and confident woman. It simply means that there will be unique challenges that both the father and daughter will face. The following is a list of tips based on a survey conducted with over 200 men who are single and raising teenage daughters. From that survey, the following tips were highlighted in no particular order:

➢ Show Respect to her Mother

This rule should go without saying. Based on my survey, having a good relationship with the mother of your daughter is beneficial because it helps with understanding the emotions and changes teenage girls go through. It also shows your young and impressionable daughter that you can be cordial with the opposite sex even when things don't work out the way you thought they would. Lastly, it takes the "family stress" levels down and as we mentioned earlier, family issues are a leading stressor for teenage girls.

➤ Give her Room to Make Mistakes

This was a common theme presented in the survey of single dads. As parents, all we want to do is shield our children from the craziness in this world. We don't want to see them go through the same things that we have gone through. However, mistakes are inevitable. Unfortunately, you cannot shield your teenager from heart break or even prevent awkward moments, you just have to be there for her when these things occur. This will create a strong bond between yourself and your teenage daughter. Additionally, she will learn to trust you.

➤ Love on Her

Most little girls idolize their fathers because they are the first loves of their life. Dads, your teenage daughter needs that love and attention specifically from you. Tell her she's beautiful and smart often. This prevents your daughter from looking for love in all the wrong places. Additionally, she will be less likely to deal with men who wish her ill will or harm because of the love and affection she received from her father.

➤ Spend time with her doing things you know She enjoys

If you know your daughter enjoys reading a good novel every once in a while, encourage her to write her own. Based on the results of the survey, single dads found that when they did things their daughter enjoyed, their daughter felt more comfortable opening up and communicating effectively. This also promotes independence within your teenage daughter. Once she finds something she is good at and that she loves, she can become the best at it. I know it is easier said than done. It is easier to just make your daughter do what you want her to do but in the long run, it will not be beneficial to you or her.

➤ Try to Learn the Developmental Process

This may be uncomfortable, but it is necessary. Understanding what your teenage daughter is going through (at least try to) will help you be a better parent. As a single dad, I know talking about your teenage daughters changing body may be cringe worthy. Talking about monthly cycles and other bodily functions is generally left up to the mother. However, if you are a single dad, you may not have this luxury, so learn! You will not regret it.

➤ Inspire her with Examples of Strong Women

This is important. Social media and various television shows can sometimes depict women in a negative way. So, it is up to you to show your teenage daughter examples of strong women. Thankfully, there are a lot to choose from like Michelle Obama, Beyonce, and probably her aunt or female cousin. Studies show that when teenagers surround themselves by strong women, they pick up on those things and become strong women themselves. Search within your immediate circle of influence including neighbors, sisters, cousins, coworkers, etc. for women willing to devote a few hours in order to provide proper guidance from a female perspective.

➢ Teach Her to Be a Problem Solver

This is a great tip. If you teach your daughter to be a problem solver, she will more than likely feel more comfortable to make sound decisions when you are not around. I would go even further and say teach her a few skills. For example, teach your daughter how to change a tire. One of the single dads on my survey admitted to teaching his daughter how to change a tire early so she would never have to wait on any man to do it.

➢ Choose your Battles Wisely

Not every argument needs to be an argument. For single dads, your daughters are seemingly perfect. So, when she acts less than perfect in your eyes, it frustrates you. I get it. However, we are all bound to make human mistakes. Sometimes, taking the high road is best when trying to raise your teenage daughter into a strong woman.

➢ Set Reasonable Expectations and Hold her Accountable

Research shows that setting reasonable expectations will allow your teenager to feel more confident about reaching her goals. A goal-oriented teenager is a teenager that is focused on her future. Fathers, you must also hold your teenager accountable. If she says she was going to reach a goal by a certain time and did not, hold her accountable by coming up with a plan to complete her goal in a reasonable manner. Additionally, hold yourself accountable. If your teenage daughter sees you are setting reasonable goals and holding yourself accountable, she will likely do the same.

➤ Join A support Group

Every single dad is not fortunate enough to have a sister or an aunt who can assist him or provide him with tips on raising his teenage daughter. Support groups can be extremely helpful. These support groups will help single fathers meet likeminded people. Additionally, support groups can assist single dads with finding positive role models and mentors for their daughters.

➤ Do not be Afraid to ask for Help

Parenthood is no easy feat. Even the most experienced parents will tell you that parenting is not for the weak hearted. We understand that fathers are not invincible. Contrary to popular belief, asking for help is not something you should be ashamed of. During those times when you just do not understand what your teenager is going through, do not be afraid to reach out to a family member for help. In addition to family members, there are government assisted programs single fathers may qualify for. Single fathers can attain help by making extensive use of government programs.

These programs will typically provide financial help for single parents. Also, online resources can be helpful. Since the percentage of single fathers raising kids on their own is lower than the percentage of single mothers, much of what is available on the web is for single and married mothers. There are not a lot of online resources targeted specifically for single dads, however, they are still helpful. These resources often give an outline on raising children, challenges faced by single parents and many more tips which might be of help for single fathers (Pace, 2020).

➢ Allow Financial Advice

Most men feel it is their duty to provide financially for their children. It is embedded in them. Life as a single father raising a teenager can be overwhelming for even the most seasoned father. Consulting with a financial advisor will assist with managing your money. Additionally, this can be an opportunity to teach your daughter about money management.

That's a Wrap!

Research suggests that more and more fathers are taking on a more active role in the lives of their children. The relationship children have with their fathers can impact the relationship they have not only with other people, but themselves as well. Children with an involved father have also been known to have higher self-control, self-discipline, social competence and empathy (Krisch, 2020). No matter how much parents detest it, the teenage years and the reckless emotions that come with those years are inevitable. Teen development is important for fathers to understand because if you understand why your teenage daughter acts a certain way, you will know how to deal with the different behaviors and emotions she will display in a positive way.

Today my daughter is in her mid-twenties, out of college and off on her own in the wild blue yonder experiencing life. Of course, it goes without saying that as her dad, I will always be concerned. The truth is though, I'm no longer afraid. She has grown into a very thoughtful, capable, intelligent, confident and independent young woman. Raising her from the age of thirteen on my own was not ideal, but if can get through it successfully, so can you.

References

Clinic, C. (2020). *Adolescent Development*
Csikszentmihalyi, M. (n.d.). *Adolescence.*
Gills, M. (2020). *Cyberbullying on rise in US*
Hemmen, L. (2012). *Parenting Teen Girls.*
Johnson, S. (2018). *Teenage Developmental Milestones: Guide to a Child's Adolescence Years.*
Jones, J., & Mosher, W. (2013). *Fathers' Involvement With Their Children: United States, 2006–2010.*
Krisch, J. A. (2020). *The Science of Dad and the 'Father Effect*
Livingston, G., & Parker, K. (2019). *8 facts about American dads*
Magher, M. (2017). *What Are the Top Ten Stressors for Teens?*
Markman, A. (2017). *How Personality Changes in Teens.*
Myers, K. (2019). *TYPICAL ISSUES DADS HAVE WHEN RAISING TEEN GIRLS.*
Pace, R. (2020). *7 Tips For Single Fathers For Raising Their Child Alone.*
Rice, A. (2020). *Raising Your Daughter as a Single Dad.*
Staff, M. C. (2020). *Tween and teen health.*
Watson, J. (2019). *aspiroadventure.com.*
Zuckerman, A. (2020). *61 SINGLE PARENT STATISTICS*